The Hearing

Kerry Shawn Keys

Cover and drawings by
Frank Miller

Paco Books

Set in Palatino on a Macintosh.

Typography and composition by Cecil Brooks.
Cover Design and drawings by Frank Miller.

First Edition

ISBN 1-879294-01-X

Paco Books
distributed by
Warm Spring Press
P.O. Box 5199
Harrisburg, PA 17110

For
Juan Antonio

and
Margarita Pavón Velasquez

Acknowledgements: Poems in this book have appeared in *Drawn and Quartered, El Heraldo, Passaic County Community College Poetry Center Anthology, Tabula Rasa, Windhorse Review,* and on WITF-FM Radio, "Verbatim."

Other books by the author: *Swallowtails Gather These Stones* (Kanchenjunga Press, 1973); *Jade Water* (Kanchenjuga Press, 1974); *O Pintor E O Poeta, Jose Paulo Moreira da Fonseca* (Spala, 1976); *Loose Leaves Fall* (Pine Press, 1977); *Quingumbo, Nova Poesia Norte-Americana* (Escrita, 1980); *A Knife All Blade,* translation of João Cabral de Melo Neto's poem, *"Uma faca só lâmina"* (Pine Press; New Directions Anthology, 44, 1982); *Death and Life of Severino, The Migrant,* translation of Cabral's verse-play, *Morte E Vida Severina* (in manuscript); *A Gathering of Smoke, Gopiah's South Indian Prose-Poem Journals* (P. Lal, Calcutta, 1986; Three Continents Press, 1989); *Blues In Green, Brazilian Poems* (Warm Spring Press, 1992).

When they make a wasteland they call it peace.

> Calgacus, *The Agricola*

Mejor ser cabeza de ratón que cola de león.

> An old proverb

Copán Ruinas . . . sacrificial altars . . . one particular altar [with] carved out receptacle for the heart, channels curving down the surface so that if one looked down upon the thing, it seemed like a yin/yang affair.

> Frank Miller, *Drawn and Quartered*

SONG: DYE ME DEER-WOMAN

Dye me deer-woman
in Autumn
a pokeweed scarf
of angora and lamb.

And should I be gone
in Winter,
wear it for me,
Love, to keep our blood warm.

Dye me deer-woman
in Autumn
a pokeweed scarf
of angora and lamb.

And though I'll be gone
in Winter—
when the snow shines,
Love, sing me this blue song.

CONTENTS

Cuando fuiste novia mía
en la primavera blanca
los cascos de tu caballo
cuatra suspiros de plata.

La luna es un pozo chico
las flores no valen nada
lo que valen son tus brazos
cuando de noche me abrazan.

Por donde irás andando
con tu cintura entallada
quiero un rico pan moreno
en el sueño de tu almohada.

La luna es un pozo chico
las flores no valen nada
lo que vale son tus brazos
cuando de noche me abrazan.

—a Zorongo Gitano

SUIT

May prayer always be spoken by rogues
and answered by silence.

Keep thunder behind the lightning
and the heart in its medieval furnace.

Burn all beatific visions
and flood the houses of the rich.

Let the game slip from the hand
and the goal go up in smoke.

Move in different directions at the same time
and fart in the face of Hope.

Put the past in the present
and the future in forgetfulness.

Cross yourself each time you slip
into skepticism or bed.

And save the flesh for love,
passion, and rebellion.

THE HORNS THAT WERE EMPTY IN THE ITALIAN GARDEN
CAFE IN TEGUCIGALPA, A PROGRESSION, 1988
for Anibal

The horns were empty, were undeciphered glyphs,
were velvet and coffee and bread
until mammals with Mayan eyebrows
blew them, turning into smoke and tortillas
circling the concrete trees with blood.

The horns were empty, were shells, until they
flattened the pitch of the coonhound's crystal bark,
cracked the red, white, and blue notes
with three chords fed on beans and wood,
with three songs fed on turtle eggs and oysters.

Minotaurs with elephant T-shirts invaded Coralio in March,
shooting up white sugar with skunk cabbage
along crystal streams of Yuscaran
where tramp-fruiters freelance bananas
and cigars for the sextons of death.

How will the horns of Pan's angels in a Hell
always in season escort the immortals
from prison to mountain, blowing trumpets,
sucking wisdom from the leaves of books,
sandbagging the red-eyed smog with fire and poems.

The empty horns are inside the absent jukebox,
are the velvet blue notes of the kiss of death,
and General Angel Chagas is pouring Coca-Cola
on his brother, Lempira, belly-up in the cafe's aquarium
where everyone's waiting for the green flash of the goldfish to set.

MANIFESTO PERDITION

Who knows where we've been today,
our legs lost at different ends
of the spectrum before having gotten there,

and there are flies on the wall
climbing over the graffiti,
and a lizard trying to catch the dot
over the i.

I could tell you more. About the man
with the gun for an oar
trying to row his boat
across delicious, lotus-filled waters

to the shore where he set off from,
but having no means to make do
he sets the dead stars on fire

and like you and you and you
he kills you and you and you.

EXPERTISE

Guard-dog.
Can it catch a rat,
kill a tick on its back?

TEGUCIGALPA

Even though starlight stinks all day reined
in the river's grey thirst, and the campesino near the Maya
hour on hour squashes the lizard with the red tail, Hell
has no mercy and the Yankee embassy is a barbwire fortress,
and the pharmacies and pizza parlors and guns
the stunned flowers and streetlights of this city,

even though Don Quixote is a professor of English Literature
in a country where the best sauce of the poor is their hunger,
and Cervantes and Morazán are exiles in Managua,
          and the brothels
have names like White House, Volcano, and Crocodile,

yes, despite this, you are here with me, my Mayan palomino,
what blessed lion's love for any lamb could tender this
softness, beautiful woman with such strange eyebrows,
          such grace,
tiny congo pepper burning our cover, making me weep all over,
o woman, white clouds and sun, moon's dove bending me home
all camouflaged in this smoke and border-crossing,
          this martyrdom.

And I will call you Tegucigalpa, city and host transformed.
Te amo, Tegucigalpa, galloping toward I know not what myth
of creation. Te amo, posted behind you, proud palomino, balm
and buttress the white cowried saddle of your cheeks, the chase
of your kiss lifting me high into your hills, O Mistress,
where the heart heals the soul's pilgrim sorrow.

Your hills, Tegucigalpa, where the cantering, mysterious starlight
still flowers, and red-tailed lizard and blue-tailed lizard
dance bit by bit together, and all the embassies of the world,
the pharmacies and guns, are demijohns of firecrackers
and candles celebrating our deep midnight's sun.

THE INQUISITION

for Victor Daniel Suazo Aragón
Miguel Angel Pavón
Moisés Landaverde
victims of the Dirección Nacional de Investigaciones, Honduras

"Hay muertos que no mueren nunca" —Jorge Luis Oviedo

Crabs are in the eddies
on the beach: orange shells
with pliars and hooks. Investigating
the tide because it turns, mutilating
the moon because it's a poor idealist,
romantic, not afraid to walk the debris
of the streets, the cemeteries of the sea at night.
When the moon's opened, look out. Scooping
out the marrow, Dionysus overboard,
there are no words to describe it: the moon
in a two-dimensional stupor above the sea,
drunken polyp, body-snatchers ready
to plug it full of botulism and obsidian bullets.

Books can tell you all about it:
the moon's grey hairs of light, the altar-stone at Copán,
fishblood and ivy running off the table,
men wrapped and burnt in the newsprint
of their own obituaries, so as not to confuse
fact with fiction, these times with those.

But who can tell you
about the thread of life, the vine

that hangs from the toothless mouth
like dental-floss, the penis cut in half,
bloody as the guts of a fish,
sea gulls yanking at it.
And who can tell you
where the maze ends, when endlessly reeling
you find your way across as if in a dream
to another shore, on your belly, like a dead ray
in a rip-tide of gleaming light. No crabs this time.
Instead, squads of pelicans overhead
with sunglasses and imported, polarized wings,
racing the sun for the chance
to take you piece by piece on a roller-coaster ride
down a wide, deserted, boatless beach.

CALL ME ZOPILOTE

Call me Zopilote
though a buzzard's
in the name.
Observe the ribcage
and thick torso,
the high cheekbones,
the rounded face
almost brown
and the dark hair
turning grey.
Call me Zopilote,
born outside
of your captive
"Banana Republics"
but carrying those stones,
that clay, that knife, that sun
inside you stomach,
dear Uncle Sam,
and dedicated to be
the words bursting there,
the rocket's red glare,
the wrecker's street rhetoric
in the pleasant barrios
along the Columbus streets
of your colonized cities.
Call me Zopilote,
call me anything you want,
call me the nothing,
the no comprende
of your one-tongued,
single-minded dreams.

SONNET FOR RUBÉN DARÍO

This afternoon an eagle flew over my head.
Was it you, Rubén my friend, disguised
as the symbol of my country's imperial appetite.
I don't think so. Daydreaming nightmares, I hear that eerie call
praising the sky's freedom; and the gifted eyes making the mistake
of staring down the European gun
as if it were a shining ray of the sun.
Sadly, the truth is I have trouble seeing any eagle,
so much has come down between. And I hope, Rubén,
this is not some silly game of reincarnation.
No eagle ever meant much to me, except its rarity
and what it once was outside written history.
That voraciousness, great size, and awful beauty
pale before the song sparrow outside my window.

FOR ARISTOPHANES

"who knows whether to live is to die"

Frogs here also, but the funnybones are on strike.
Donkeys on their backs. Reporters in the Ritz.
In the markets, toads get exercise in the afternoon
gargling goldenseal and red pepper powder.
Rain brings out some, others go in.
What's it like to be stuffed with something
other than bugs, Paco lectures, like shit
and the newspapers and endless books. Paco points—
maybe you're a spy, maybe we're bugged.
There's a scorpion in the bathroom,
brown tail touching the torch,
and the birds on the bayou at San Lorenzo
watch the marines embark from their ship
and enter the small, entrepreneurship of a brothel
nicknamed Casa Blanca. It's where the exiles
from the Crocodile in the capital come to service
the gringos and distribute Aids for free—
peace corps largess in reverse.
Then there's the salted, green mangoes, assholes,
and other sorts of catholic charity
the troops usually come across—
according to the banal reports in the newspapers
about these "third-world, banana countries."

CAROUSING WITH PACO, LÊDO, AND RUBÉN DARÍO

Tonight's the night the ants
are drinking our urine.

COMPROMISED

Hunting insects, the legs crack
a long time around the clock.
Bees bathed in pollen,
the anther the stinger. Ants
sizzling in the thunder of murder
outside the ant-trees
in the holocaust of the tormented sun.
Beetles squashed into green syllables
on the sidewalks where Jack loves Jill.
Flies smeared above the bed
with sperm and snot. Wasps and spiders
desiccated gladiators in jars.
Fireflies for wedding rings. Butterfly wings
under glass. Moths lured by nightlights
to their deathly identification. Words win.
End of first stanza.
Stanza two. In Nicaragua, the againsts
drink fruitflies with their calala.
And the fors who are also againsts
—against the Yankees—try their best
not to turn into cockroaches
and swarm with the black ants
around the filthy toilets in Masaya.
The in-betweens dance reggae on the Blue Coast.
If you go to the other coast
someday during stanza three,
be sure to visit the Hotel Summer.
Water rationing, free mosquitoes
buzz from the showerheads
to sip tourist blood all night,
laughing and carrying on as if it were
some rich, dark aphrodisiac. It is.
Once a week Somoza sleepwalks from the dead,
squeezing lime juice in the urinals,

slurping oysters, reading the Wall Street Journal.
The Ortega brothers stick toothpicks
in his balls pretending they're olives.
Violeta gives him a blow-job
while stuffing the last stanza of this poem
in his mouth. So the rumors fly. So the world turns,
so the dying are recycled circles, insects and humans.
So death with its ends gone, turns to eat.

TWO FUNERALS: MANAGUA AND HARRISBURG

for Donaldo Altamirano

The ants look like bright young cadets
pallbearing the lizard away.
There's no heavy coffin, and yet
its body seems as stiff as wood,
and they're working up a sweat
in their regimented, moonlit march.
This is their graveyard, warzone shift.
They will take it home to hang and then
dispatch in their suburban gallery at noon.

I carried my father's coffin to the grave.
When they lowered him into the ground
I thought I heard the ants and worms
thanking me for the free delivery.
They promised me to eat him more slowly
since they had hardly worked up a hunger.
And they told me because he had never been a soldier
not to cry in public and not to make a film about it.

HEARSAY

According to a Latin American poet,
and this has nothing to do
with the time of day or the season,
but is written in the stars,
we must save men and women
from so much injustice, use them
as examples without an Inquisition
in an all out assault on the mansions
of Heaven, but people are born
down and out, and die alone in the woods
in isolation with insanity as a birthmark
where there's no room for mercy
or the ax or heresy . . .
                              but
the axes are everywhere, parakeets
flutter in and out of the toxic fumes
of the Boca del Infierno crater.
There's plenty of room
for each cut tree/leaves a little more sunshine
to bleach the bones, to scour and scan
the useless, acid-free books
of second-hand poets and firsts. It bleaches
the sheets of hungry lovers. It bleaches
the pupils of the dead.

THE MISSING

Nothing to do with black holes.
Nothing to do with potholes.
Missing is to have a pothole
in the guts, black hole for a heart.
To be blind, not to know if someone
sees you or not.
It's a no knife, a no flower, a no egg.
Missing is to be the bones of the guapote.

                    guapote—a succulent, "boneless" fish found
                        in Lake Nicaragua

IDENTIFICATION

Sir, your passport please.
When a bird flies through the air
where are its footprints.

I said, Sir, your passport.
When I held her goodbye, breath
on her hair, the wind took with her
all memory of other desire.

You can't enter this country, Sir,
if you don't comply with the regulations.
I've complied with the dark,
licked clean as a light
with no leaf to shine in.

Come this way.
Daylight, Sir, is an animal
stuck in a circle of snow and mud. Blood
for ink, stencils for eyes. My feet
are not mine. Color of heart: blind.

There is a problem, Hombre, you can't leave
without name or passport.
Without roots or dreams, there's no problem
of coming or going. I am where I am.
Today I saw a stuffed frog under glass,
a uniform with a gun, purple flowers,
and a stone turtle in the park.

unused tropes . . . tamales, tapas, Yuscaran, dead of night outside the barroom, banana peels, whores in the brothels across the river in the Heavenly City. Mariachis and Elvis on the jukebox. Not one good woman or one good line to bring on the dawn. What town? underfoot. Not one . . . to bed down with, no see never nancite in the guaro, the small, round yellow fruit soaking the spirits under the silk cotton trees. Clay rooster on the desk back at the Hotel Iberia. Somewhere, though, up in the hills, maybe near crazy Juana's house, there's a cock drunk on imported Flor de Caña in the backroom of a poolhall, testing out a filibuster because he's not ready for the block, and another poet and another flamenco guitarist shooting turtle eggs across green felt while firecrackers of pigeons shingle suddenly into dark-blue patterns across the cobbled sky matching the balls going down smooth, dark rails into burning, endlessly devout pockets . . . somewhere up in the hills there's a radiant rooster perched on a mile-high eucalyptus tree relishing the starlight and listening to the mangoes falling on the tin roofs far away in Managua, and keeping an eye on the giant, leather frogs, the bronze, dismembered horse, the star-broken starfruit, the guitar hanging in the window next to the gun leaning on the sill at the DNI hangout called the Picnic . . . and that rooster is also drunk on caña, and there's Paco and O'Henry and another poet shooting turtle eggs, etc., he seems to be me breaking open the triangle.

TELA

durante su ausencia

The play of darkness persists, the textured
cutlass of lights on the Caribbean.
Cool. Interbreeding. Lila, loka, lavation.
Tela. Tela. Tela. What is the heart fed,
where is that ocean, that mangrove of other darkness?

Spring has come. The clear bells of Los Dolores ring
their long ride here, and lay down a laurencian air over the bay.
The wild orchid tree's in bloom. Your body swaying
in the first heat of Spring smells like a wild orchid,
blossoms like an Iberian almond, and I know
dying all the time that I'm dancing with you
at my own wake, putting the candle out behind,
a glory of Garifuna songs cheering me on.

                                        Darkness comes again
to interrupt the rhythm, that black ceramic lizard,
and the uncanny moon soon cakewalks over the ocean
behind another tune, turning the drums
          and mantras and magpies
to stone as in a moment of stone, that moment when we see
our bones as our sisters, our tintype, smiling face
the postponed parrot of certain oblivion.

Only hours away in the mountains, tobacco smoke
rains down the ruins at Copán. Scribes
are seated to the right of their daily selves—innocent,
numbered abstractions—while on the beach here
the ocean swamps over the Lean River
that came from the hills so far away to meet her, a lovers' tryst,
swamps the shattered shells and red, pestled stones, ignores
the desperate, distant altars as stars ignore astronomers,

as fish ignore the power brokers and priests of corn.
The hammock swings, a metronome counterpoint to
Arawakan angels' wings of sand, and the colorless blood of sleep
furiously rolls down the shades.
                              Tela, the salt-pools
of your arched, Mayan eyebrows, the African beat of crow's-feet
tracking your imagined laughter along the beach,
are the heart's true hieroglyphics
linking the peeling play of light in the palm trees,
the semantics of the quiet snail at the tide's lips,
and the coconut's ground swell of golden rum.

GROOT-ZUNDERT IN THE TROPICS

Magpies nesting
in the blue acacia.
Kike's Dry Cleaners down the street,
the bay at Tela—
waking up in the morning
to the twittering shrieks,
going to sleep to the same
squeaking machine, thinking
of Van Gogh, of Provence, of old Blue Jay,
my good ear to the pillow,
the other ear highjacked
half-way to India, a wild flower
pressed into the pages of the Koran.

IN THE DARKNESS OF MY PALM

Blossoms of the peach tree
have fallen silently
to earth. No one has heard
better than I who have seen them.
The small birds have returned
from the burning mountains of Managua
where rings of rust
cloud the shell-shocked moon.
One by four at nightfall stars appear,
the souls of dead moths and men
free at last from the sun.

Walking through the mint and parsley
and weeds in the garden,
I carry a glowworm in the darkness
of my palm, looking for a woman
who will love me honestly forever,
however so often I go down
to the dark-rose river alone.